Dinosa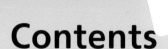

Contents

Written by
Emma Lynch

When did they live?

Apatosaurus

Stegosaurus

Dinosaurs **reigned** a long time ago. We know this because their **fossils** are found all over the Earth.

Brachiosaurus

Oviraptor

We can't know for sure how many kinds of dinosaurs there were. So far, scientists have found around 300!

What were they like?

Dinosaurs had dry, wrinkly skin. Most
dinosaurs had big bodies and little brains.
They laid eggs in nests on the ground.

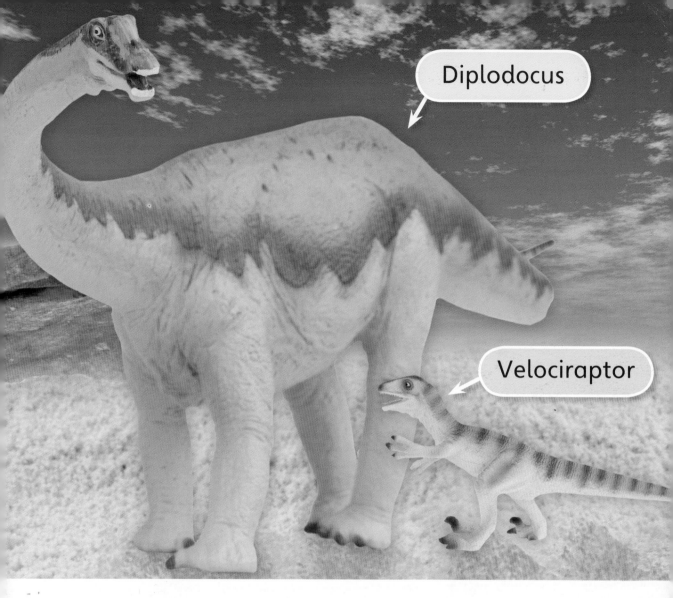

Some dinosaurs ran on just two legs.
Some needed all four limbs for balance.

Big and little

Apatosaurus was so big that you would
have to climb high just to reach its knee!

Compsognathus

Compsognathus was no bigger than a new-born lamb!

Food

Tyrannosaurus Rex

Tyrannosaurus Rex was a meat eater – it guzzled small animals. It even gobbled up little dinosaurs!

Apatosaurus had a long neck so it could reach the treetops.

Some dinosaurs were plant eaters – they didn't eat meat at all.

Teeth, spikes and claws

Dinosaurs had sharp teeth to **gnaw** their food. Oviraptor had two spikes in its mouth to crack open dinosaurs' eggs.

Velociraptor had claws as sharp as knives to help it wrestle and kill its prey.

Diplodocus would lash its tail like a whip if it was tackled in a fight.

Without its tail,
Diplodocus could
be knocked over.

Stegosaurus had sharp spikes on its tail.
It used these like knives to protect itself.

Lost and found

Dinosaurs died out. We don't know why. All that is left of them is their footprints and fossils.

The bones fit together like a jigsaw puzzle.

Scientists **comb** rocky places to find dinosaur fossils.

Glossary

comb   look for very carefully

fossils   remains of an animal or plant that lived a long time ago

gnaw   bite and chew

reigned   ruled over animals (or humans)